BIPOLAR WORKBOOK

The Complete Bipolar Disorder Survival Guide to Stopping Mood Swings

(Learn the Symptoms and Strategies on How You Can Cope)

Anthony Friesen

Published by Oliver Leish

Anthony Friesen

All Rights Reserved

Bipolar Workbook: The Complete Bipolar Disorder Survival Guide to Stopping Mood Swings (Learn the Symptoms and Strategies on How You Can Cope)

ISBN 978-1-77485-091-6

Legal & Disclaimer

The information contained in this book is not designed to replace or take the place of any form of medicine or professional medical advice. The information in this book has been provided for educational and entertainment purposes only.

The information contained in this book has been compiled from sources deemed reliable, and it is accurate to the best of the Author's knowledge; however, the Author cannot guarantee its accuracy and validity and cannot be held liable for any errors or omissions. Changes are periodically made to this book. You must consult your doctor or get professional medical advice before using any of the suggested remedies, techniques, or information in this book.

Upon using the information contained in this book, you agree to hold harmless the Author from and against any damages, costs, and expenses, including any legal fees potentially resulting from the application of any of the information provided by this guide. This disclaimer applies to any damages or injury caused by the use and application, whether directly or indirectly, of any advice or information presented, whether for breach of contract, tort, negligence, personal injury, criminal intent, or under any other cause of action.

You agree to accept all risks of using the information presented inside this book. You need to consult a professional medical practitioner in order to ensure you are both able and healthy enough to participate in this program.

Table of Contents

Introduction

This book is mostly for self-help and informational purposes only. It is no way intended to replace expert and medical advice regarding bipolar disorder. If you think that you or any of your loved ones have this condition, do not limit your knowledge to the information provided in this book.

It's best to consult with a psychiatrist for primary and immediate treatment of bipolar disorder. Just make this book a supplemental reference that will help you and your loved ones cope with bipolar disorder.

Thanks again, I hope you enjoy it!

Chapter 1: What Is Bipolar Disorder?

Bipolar disorder is a specific mood disorder characterized as a mental illness by mental health experts. The mental health bible, Diagnostic and Statistical Manual, 5th edition, proposed that there are three kinds of bipolar disorders: bipolar I disorder, bipolar II disorder, and cyclothymic disorder. These forms are differentiated on the level of severity of the problem.

Basically, what these three forms have in common is that an individual with this disorder experiences episodes of extreme mania and extreme depression during their lifetime. Mania and depression are considered as two opposing poles in the mood spectrum. Hence, the disorder is labeled as 'bipolar' because an individual experiences duality of affective (mood) states.

The more known aspect of bipolar disorder is depression where an individual experiences inability to find pleasure in any activities.

A person experiencing depression also feels intense sadness for no apparent reason at all. People with bipolar disorder will find oneself experiencing lack of interest in doing anything.

They are unproductive in a sense that they cannot engage themselves into doing something.

A person in a depressive episode will have a hard time waking up and getting out of the bed.

Solitude is preferred during this moments and the person will likely to veer away from any conversation.

Negative thoughts will haunt the person and feeling of unworthiness is predominant during this episode.

It can be said that the person suffering in this episode is seen surrounded with a dark aura.

The other side of bipolar disorder is mania. Opposite to depression, mania is a state of intense elation.

People having manic episode seems to find pleasure in everything, and would like to involve themselves in many activities.

They tend to be enthusiastic in doing many things, which naturally leads to unproductivity because they cannot keep their attention for one thing at a time.

A person in a manic episode is also likely to be very sociable at this time.

Other people will find it hard to keep up with a manic person and there is tendency for the person to dominate the conversation.

Everything about mania is the opposite of depression. Others who observe people in manic episode would likely describe the person to be chaotic. There is also tendency for the person experiencing mania to engage in risky behaviors such as substance abuse and casual sex. Those behaviors, though, belongs most often to full-blown mania. Other manic tendencies include flight of ideas, delusions of grandeur and even psychotic tendencies.

People with bipolar disorder experiences these two extreme mood swings. There will be times that a person may act 'normally'. That would be episodes where others can say that these people are in their 'usual self'. They act without significant difference to what is acceptably normal in the society. However, when depressive episode comes in, these people will tend to shy away from others, and feel that things could never be right for them. On the manic episode, these people will be highly talkative, producing too many ideas. These people will be very active and others will see them as 'not their usual selves'. They may even be mistaken as under the influence of drugs due to their erratic behavior.

Experiencing bipolar disorder or being with a person who has bipolar disorder can be likened to riding on a roller coaster; there will be times when the mood is too high and times when the mood is too low. The inconsistency of the mood, not to mention the extremity, brings about confusion on how to deal with these people. Even those who experience this are in confusion themselves because of the inconsistency that they experience. Experiencing the extreme ups and downs is not pleasurable, and this adds more to the problem. Aside from that, productivity of these individuals who have this disorder is also in question. In conclusion, people with this disorder are seen as dysfunctional due to unproductivity and the display of behavior cannot be considered 'normal'.

Chapter 2: What Is Bipolar Disorder?

An important step in coping with any condition is to first know what it really is and what it means for you and your loved ones. First and foremost, bipolar disorder is a medical illness that can impair a person's ability to function normally. If untreated, people with bipolar disorder can find it difficult to perform routine tasks and activities, and may find their mood swings (formally known as "manias" or "depression") uncontrollable.

Someone who is bipolar will often experience incredible highs known as "manias", or incredible lows known as "depression". A midway emotional state called "hypomania" is generally positive and not as severe as the aforementioned highs and lows, but it runs the great risk of quickly turning into a manic episode or a depressive episode.

As you can imagine, shuttling between these states causes great emotional and mental distress, particularly because these are often unpredictable.

Here are some general symptoms to watch out for that most often point to bipolar disorder:

-Sudden shifts between extreme happiness and sadness; high activity to low activity levels

-Inability to see tasks through to their completion; often, the individual has a growing stack of half-finished projects and easily moves on to something else

-Lack of focus/easily distracted

-A noticeable tendency to believe in grand ideas, or to create unrealistic plans

-Depression or low mood levels

-Unusual levels of activity/ low activity

-Unusual changes in appetite and weight (loss or gain)

-Significant irritability/anger

-Rapid speech; incessant talking

-Problems in the workplace and with workload (e.g. quitting unexpectedly, unfinished tasks, hampered concentration, frequent absences/tardiness, etc.)

-Engaging in risky/dangerous behaviour (e.g. drug and alcohol abuse, reckless driving, self-harming behaviour, etc.)

-Unusual phases of euphoria and extreme elation; may involve false beliefs or psychosis (delusions or hallucinations)

-Having a flight of ideas or spikes in creativity; individuals often describe feeling overwhelmed by an uncontrollable rush of thoughts

-Having manic, hypomanic, or depressive episodes (these will be discussed later on)

While these may not immediately mean that your loved one is struggling with bipolar disorder, they are red flags that may point to the presence of the condition.

In the case that your loved one has been diagnosed with bipolar disorder, you will need to watch out for episodes of mania, hypomania, or depression.

Chapter 3: Bipolar Disorder And Suicide

It can be pretty difficult to live with bipolar disorder; you often feel emotionally and physically drained, you feel like you have lost control of your own mind, and you feel as if you will not get better for the rest of your life. The mental anguish that almost all bipolar patients go through can be so severe that suicidal thoughts are nothing new to them.

Having bipolar disorder not only makes people more prone to taking their own lives, it actually makes them want to kill themselves in the most violent way they can think of. Most of the time, sufferers will have hallucinations of how they want to die, but not actually have any compulsions to go through with the suicide attempt. It is when people go through particularly bad depressive episodes that people take their lives.

Suicide can be a touchy subject when you are talking about bipolar disorder, but you need to know their correlation nonetheless. You need to catch yourself before you actually think about taking your own life because you cannot stand not being in control of your emotions. This chapter is not meant to scare, in fact, you need to know how to prevent suicidal thoughts from even coming into your mind so you can stop yourself, or someone like you, before it is too late.

Why Do Bipolar Disorder Patients Get Suicidal Thoughts?

What is it about suicidal thoughts that make them so appealing for bipolar disorder patients? This is the thing that runs through the minds of people who have no idea of what's it like to go through severe bipolar episodes. Other people do not know the kind of mental strain people like you have to go through; how it can be so mentally draining that it can place the patient in an almost catatonic state and there is nothing he/she can do about it once it starts.

After going through such a horrible mental ordeal, the thoughts of just ending it all seems like a breath of fresh air. Patients who have bipolar disorder are already sick and tired of the extreme mood swings that they get, and it only gets much worse when they go through a depressive episode. A startling statistic about bipolar disorder is that 25% to 50% of sufferers are found out to have attempted to end their lives at least once. You need to learn more about suicidal thoughts and its relationship with bipolar disorder if you do not want to become a contributor to that horrible statistic.

Warning Signs

There are several things that you need to keep an eye out for if you are worried that your bipolar disorder may lead you to commit suicide - here are some of the more common ones:

•When you find yourself actually talking about killing yourself

•Always thinking about how you are going to die

•Often feeling that you are worthless and hopeless

•You find yourself doing reckless stuff that you would not normally do

•You take irrational risks, as if you are actually defying death

•You suddenly wanted to make/revise your last will and testament

•You suddenly get the urge to settle all the important things right away; like taking a time deposit or signing up for life insurance to make sure that your son/daughter will be well taken care of in the event that you were to suddenly disappear

•Your depressive episodes seem to get worse every time it comes

When you see these signs manifest in you then you need to get in touch with the people closest to you and actually tell them that you are planning on committing suicide. You should never ever keep suicidal thoughts bottled up inside of you; always confide in another person so you will be able to rebound and beat these evil thoughts before they take over your mind completely. You can also call your local suicide helpline so you can have someone to talk to and provide you with insight as to why taking your own life is not the answer to your problems.

Although having bipolar disorder makes you more prone to suicide, it does not mean that you have to go through with it. You just need to catch yourself when you are beginning to consider this horrible option.

Chapter 4: Signs & Symptoms

Individuals experiencing bipolar disorder often experience symptoms called mood episodes. These are noticeable moments when different emotional states happen. These emotional states are usually intense or extreme episodes. Unfortunately, bipolar disorder is a lifelong disorder and the episodes can usually go away, but come back after a long or short period of time. Individuals that are in between episodes may be free of symptoms, while others may persistent and lasting symptoms.

There are four basic distinct types of episodes that are prevalent in individuals suffering from bipolar disorder; manic episodes, hypomania, depressive episodes. In the most severe cases, these episodes can occur almost simultaneously, and is labeled as a mixed state.

What is a Depressive Episode? A depressive episode is a mood disorder that is often exemplified by a prevalent and persistent sad or low mood. This low mood is usually accompanied by a drop in confidence and self-esteem and by a loss of interest in one's favorite or gratifying activities. Depressive episodes in bipolar disorder is the same as clinical depression. Symptoms of a Depressive Episode:

•Extended amount of time feeling sad or extremely disheartened.

•No longer interested in your much-loved activities.

•Poor concentration

•Extreme indecisiveness or inability to make decisions.

•Frequent suicidal thoughts or attempts.

•Frequent restlessness and irritability

•Sudden changes in sleep patterns, eating habits, and other habits.
•Tiredness

•Suicidal thoughts

Symptoms of a Depressive Episode in Children:

•Experience small amounts of energy and displays little to no interest in fun activities

•Shows a significantly increased or decreased appetite

•Sleeps way too long or frequently

•Does not sleep enough

•Frequent pains like headaches or stomach pains

•Frequent feelings of guilt

What is a Manic Episode?

A manic episode is completely opposite of a depressive episode, and changes erratically.
Maniac episodes usually last for a period of at least 1 week, and is characterized by elevated, extensive irritability mood or abnormal persistence in reaching goals. Symptoms of a Manic Episode:

•Intense happy or gregarious moods.

•Provocative, hostile, or aggressive behavior

•Frequent restlessness and agitation

•Constant involvement in impulsive and high risk behaviors

•Impracticable belief in your own capabilities

•Taking on an unrealistically amount of work, projects, or responsibilities

•Easily distracted

•Racing thoughts

•Frequently changing from one idea to another

•Talking awkwardly fast

Symptoms of a Manic Episode in Children:

•Lacks the ability to focus or stay on task

•Talks or thinks about sexually explicit things frequently

•Experiences troubles sleeping, but not tired

•Partakes in hazardous actions

•Has a very short temper

•Extreme, but unusual feelings of happiness

•Unusual acts of silliness

What is Hypomania?

Hypomania is a less extreme version of a mania.
In a hypomanic state, one may experience feelings of euphoria and energy. However, carry on with day to day tasks is not a problem. People experiencing a hypomanic episode often make decisions that harm their

careers, relationships, reputations, and finances.

Symptoms of a Hypomanic State:

•Reckless actions and no concern for the after effects or consequences

•Impulsiveness or terrible decision making

•Easily distracted

•Inability to concentrate

•Unusually optimism or unrealistic belief in one's capabilities.
•Rapid change of thoughts

•Experience severe delusions or hallucinations

What is a Mixed State?

A mixed state is usually an episode that is a mix of depression and mania. Mixed states can last for an unusually extended amount of time, or can happen in a very short sequence. For example, while in a mixed state one may feel awfully sad or useless, but have a fullness of energy at the same time.

Symptoms of a Mixed State:

•Taking on an unrealistically amount of work, projects, or responsibilities

•Fatigue and restlessness

•Extreme feelings of guilt

•Intense paranoia

•Easily distracted

•Racing thoughts

•Frequently changing from one idea to another

•Talking awkwardly fast

•Repeated thoughts of death

Symptoms of a Mixed State in Children:

•Frequent feelings of guilt

•Experiences troubles sleeping, but not tired

•Has a very short temper

•Talks or thinks about sexually explicit things frequently

•Lacks the ability to focus or stay on task

•Easily distracted

•Experience small amounts of energy and displays little to no interest in fun activities

•Poor concentration

These are some of the key symptoms and signs that people with bipolar disorder

usually   display.
If these episodes become too severe, the
symptoms can easily become psychotic or
over embellished.   For example, if your
depressive state is too extreme, one might
have the feeling that you have done
something extreme like kill someone or
committed a crime or are extremely poor.
Those   experiencing   intense   maniac
episodes   my
feel like you are a renowned, extremely
rich, or famous person or that you might
be   a   superhero   or   have   special
superhuman powers.

Chapter 5: Natural Products That Can Fight Bpd

For those that do not trust, or do not want to undergo the traditional medical avenues, there are natural products that can be very helpful as remedies to BPD. It is recommended that before using any of the herbs and oils in the list, to consult the attending medical specialist, as some of them may have harmful side effects. Here is what can be used against bipolar disorder:

1) St. Johns' Wort

This is a known anti-depressant herb. During the manic phase of the disorder anti-depressants of all kinds are not to be taken. There is also an issue of dosage, as excessive use may trigger the manic phase. Do not use before consultation with your doctor.

2)Flaxseed oil

This is also a kind of natural anti-depressant containing alpha-linolenic acid (ALA). It is ideal to be combined with traditional medical compounds addressing people who suffer from anxiety caused by the bipolar disorder. It is not considered as a standard treatment, but the relevant research shows that it is very helpful in combination with traditional medicine.

3)Ginseng

This herb is extremely helpful in improving memory, attention and concentration levels. It is recommended for patients that after the depression episode, experience fatigue and lethargy.

4) Gingko Biloba

It is an extract from the ginko tree and improves memory functionality along with being an antioxidant which helps the blood circulation in the brain. Best results are obtained if the herb is consumed during the depression phase regularly and for a period of eight to twelve weeks.

5)Black Cohosh

Also known as black snakeroot or squaw root. It is a depressant of the nervous system and a sedative as well as anti-inflammatory. It is useful over a period of time which is to be discussed with the attending physician as prolonged usage may cause liver problems.

6)Valerian Root

This is a strong sedative which is also used in the treatment of various anxiety disorders. Used regularly it promotes a feeling of calmness and reduces all stress related contributing factors. It is also most helpful for those that experience sleeping problems and headaches.

7)Licorice

This herb promotes the production of hormones present in the brain. BPD patients should drink a cup of licorice tea daily. It is most effective against the depression phase of bipolar disorder.

8)Passionflower

The main contribution of passionflower is the balancing of the neurotransmitters in the brain. Its sedative properties are helpful during the manic phase of BPD and against insomnia. A side effect of the use of passionflower is upsetting the stomach.

As amply displayed there is quite a number of natural products that can help people suffering from bipolar disorder through its different phases. But this is only the first part of the equation. In the flowing chapters you will find the other parts that will produce the =BPD overcome result.

Chapter 6: Myths On Borderline Personality Disorder

BPD is a mental illness often misunderstood by the general population and even some health care practitioners. BPD is also known as BPD. It is also a disease that can have a detrimental impact on the lives of others. There are many myths about BPD because of these two problems. It is so imperative to understand the truth about the disease if you or someone you know is BPD to begin recovery. Below are some of the most common BPD myths.

Myth 1: Untreatable Borderline Personality Disorder

This is entirely false; BPD can be treated. Do not let this myth frighten you from therapy if you think you have BPD, or make you feel helpless.

A diagnosis does not mean you will experience BPD symptoms forever. Hard work and efficient treatment can reduce BPD symptoms significantly and can help you to live a healthy life.

Even without treatment, symptoms of the disorder will ebb and flow over time; some people with BPD can function more effectively than others.

Myth 2: All People with BPD Are Victims of Childhood Abuse

All too often, people of good intentions who do not understand BPD believe it is due to childhood abuse. This can change how people interact with you or speak with you if you have BPD, which can be frustrating if you have no damage. It may feel like it is not understood or different for your own experience. While some people who have BPD have been abused, this is not true for all patients with BPD and should be seen with a more open mind.

Till this present minute, there is no known cause of BPD. The cause is generally regarded instead of being linked to anyone's cause as a combination of biological and environmental factors.

Myth 3: Adults and Children Cannot Be Diagnosed with Bipolar Personality Disorder

With BPD, children and adolescents cannot be diagnosed with borderline personality disorders. However, because of the generally accepted belief that personality is still developed throughout adolescence, it was controversial to diagnose children or teens with BPD.

The fifth-edition of the Diagnostic Statistical Manual (DSM-V) sets out clear standards for the diagnosis of BPD. However, caution should be employed when making a diagnosis, particularly for BPD, as the symptoms often reflect typical teenage behavior. A professional BPD therapist can help to distinguish the difference. Early diagnosis can help to ensure that an individual receives the procedure necessary to start recovery.

Myth 4: Bipolar Personality Disorder Is A Variation Of Bipolar Disorder

Bipolar personality disorder and bipolar disorder are entirely different. While bipolar and BPD symptoms may appear somewhat similar, they are two distinct diseases.

Since even healthcare providers are unaware of BPD, people with bipolar disorder are often misdiagnosed and confused. It is as well crucial to note that drugs for the treatment of bipolar disorder often do not work for BPD patients. Therefore a BPD-based therapist must obtain a proper diagnosis and treatment plan.

Myth 5: BPD Is Found Only in Women

BPD is found in both sexes, although it is true that women are diagnosed with BPD more frequently than men.

However, this does not occur in all way and mean females are more likely to develop BPD. It may mean that males ' symptoms are linked to other diseases, such as post-traumatic stress disorder or depression, more incorrectly. The characteristics of BPD are instability and a poor pulse control, which can equally affect both sexes.

Myth 6: If You Know Someone With BPD, You Know Them in All Way

Everyone is unique, and having BPD does not change that. You know everyone.

The DSM-V standard for mental health requires specific criteria for the diagnosis of BPD. The approach covers personality impairment and interpersonal relationships. The way these impairments are shown in each adult is different.

Moreover, not all people experience specific symptoms in the same way. The difficulty of a person with relationships may be different from yours—each experience BPD in very different ways.

Problems In Diagnosis: Related and Coexisting Illnesses

Researches, in the last decade, have confirmed that BPD is much more often than was previously thought associated with other psychiatric diseases. Unlike the "Farmer in the Dell" cheese, BPD seldom stands alone. Some of the defining symptoms are identical to other disease criteria. For example, as with borderlines, many people living with ADHD show impatience, impulsivity, anger speed, broken relationships, poor self-esteem, and frequent drug abuse. An anti-social personality disorder is characterized by impulsiveness and outbursts of anger. Depression is the most common "fellow traveler" with BPD. More than 95% of BPD patients also fulfill this disorder criterion. Nearly 90 percent of frontiers also meet criteria for anxiety, particularly post-traumatic stress disorder, and panic and social anxiety disorder. Although both genders experience depression and anxiety equally, drug abuse and sociopaths are seen significantly more often on male borders, whereas eating disorders and post-traumatic stress disorders are correlated with women's boundaries more often. All these diseases are found in borderline areas much more often than with other personality disorders.

Because borders usually have several afflictions, the clinician must first address the symptoms that are the most disabled. And she must juggle the effects on accompanying problems of treatment. Many borderlines have accompanying ADHD symptoms, for example, will the borderline symptoms of rage and mood change become worse when she initiates therapy for the poor concentration and distractibility of stimulant medicine? Conversely, will she be able to maintain attention adequately to benefit from treatment if she engages the patient in intensive psychotherapy? To ensure thorough and balanced treatment, accurate diagnosis of all disorders is necessary.

BPD can also imitate other diseases. Mood changes can be misdiagnosed as bipolar disorder. Temporary psychosis may imitate schizophrenia. When an associated disorder such as depression or alcoholism is prominent, the significant underlying BPD may be camouflaged. Although BPD may accompany other diseases, distinguishing it from other complications is essential. Borderline depression and mood swings are usually associated with situational conditions and may, therefore, change within hours. Major depressive and bipolar disorders last for days or longer and may not have any interaction with events in the life of a person.

Furthermore, a person with a disorder usually works well between episodes, while the borderline can continue to conduct itself in destructive behavior. Temporary stress-related borderline psychosis may seem acutely like paranoid schizophrenia. However, psychosis in BPD is short-lived and can sometimes dissolve within hours. The schizophrenic psychotic disease is usually chronic and less associated with external stressors. While borderlines also recover from traumas, post-traumatic stress disorder (PTSD) is characterized by particularly severe crisis reactions. Recurring intrusive thinking on the event, avoiding associated sites or activities, and hyper-vigilance with over-starting responses are not typical of BPD. Physiological differences suggest that BPD patients are more responsive to abandonment issues, while PTSD patients have a more extreme response to trauma-emphasizing presentations.

Diagnostic Bias

BPD is often misdiagnosed and underdiagnosed despite its frequency. Primary care physicians, who are usually the first to be treated for psychiatric problems, can diagnose and treat BPD with precision less than half the time.

Coexisting diseases may lead in various ways to the under-diagnosis of BPD. Many clinicians ignore the diagnosis of Axis II when another disorder is primary, focusing on the treatment of Axis 1 (usually more comfortable to treat, because its focus is on medication rather than on complicated, extensive psychotherapy). Also, managed care companies sometimes discourage ongoing therapy for personality disorders, as such patients typically need more intensive–and more costly–long-term treatment. Many insurance companies would completely deny compensation for BPD, saying that the required expensive care is not part of the policy. Paradoxically, some medical case managers deny certification on the wrong assumption that restricting patients never get better, that care does not improve, and that therapy is, therefore, attempting to waste resources. Many doctors, therefore, avoid the borderline label to minimize problems with managed care companies.

Finally, because of its stigma within the profession, many clinicians are reluctant to diagnose BPD. Borderline patients are the most apprehensive among many practitioners. They have an overly demanding reputation with frequent telephone calls and attention agitation. They are the most controversial psychiatric community. When they are disappointed, their anger is hard to tolerate. Constant suicide threats can be hard to manage. The treatment requires much patience and even more time, often not adequately recognized or reimbursed in today's climate. So many BPD diagnosed patients cannot approach trained physicians who are willing to accept them in care.

Roots of BPD

Several methods have been employed to investigate the causes and roots of BPD. Family studies have confirmed that most borderlines have experienced severe developmental disturbances, indicating environmental causes.

Recent neurological and genetic researches have theorized that biological foundations may be heritable. An essential borderline subgroup has a history of perinatal or acquired brain injury.

A new research line that blends genetic/biological vulnerabilities with environmental traumas to create minimal coping mechanisms. A model suggests that hereditary (called temperament) traits interact with developmental (character) values to generate personality. So temperament + character= character= personality. Specific temperaments can also be discerned and related to biologic imbalances and sensitivities. Temperament models develop early in life and are viewed as instinctual or habitual. Character styles gradually come into being and culminate in adulthood.

Anatomical and Biological Correlates

Some of the most exciting new studies of BPD research use current health techniques to investigate the workings of the brain, such as chemical change control and the identification of anatomic changes. Some studies have shown that excessive neurotransmitter serotonin levels (a chemical that has a nerve conductivity throughout the body) may lead to an increase in BPD impulsivity and aggression. Interestingly, such sensitivity is seen more often in women, who account for 75% of borders. One study used positron emission tomography (PET) scanning in men's and women's BPD's brains to show lower levels of serotonin activity that correlated with increased impulsivity. Certain neurotransmitters such as dopamine and GABA can also be involved in the regulation of impulsive aggression. The acetylcholine and norepinephrine neurotransmitters are associated with mood modulation. Medicines to control these imbalances in neurotransmitters have been shown to reduce borderline symptoms.

Many scientists have studied the link between BPD and autoimmune disorders, where the body reacts allergically and develops antibodies against its organs. Rheumatoid arthritis, for example, is related to an unusually high incidence of BPD. One study was conducted on a woman with fluctuating BPD symptoms over nine months, while her antithyroid antibodies were measured. Such researchers found significantly lower anticody rates during times when their depression and paranoia were small, and higher when their symptoms increased. This finding indicates that autoimmune inflammation may exacerbate or vice versa BPD symptoms.

Scientists who study BPD neurology have focused on the part of the brain called the limbic system. The brain part influences memory, learning, emotional conditions (for example, anxiety), and behavior (especially aggressive and sexual). Borderline EEG analyzes have shown dysfunction in this part of the brain. One research used magnetic resonance imaging in problematic females with a trauma history to examine improvements in limbic system length. Such authors have shown significantly reduced volume in this brain zone's hippocampus and amygdala areas. This link between past physical or emotional traumas and subsequent changes in brain volume associated with frontier dysfunction increases the risk for child abuse to affect brain function, resulting in questionable actions. The course of the organization was not seen. Another explanation could be that BPD causes (instead of causing) change in the volume of the brain that is only fortuitously associated with past trauma.

Environmental and Genetic Roots

In recent years, genetic and environmental Roots genome work has exploded. Gene mapping, cloning ability, and stem cell production have created new limits of medical disease understanding and care. Certain BPD researchers have tried to determine that specific genes may be responsible for specific borderline behavior types. Identity instability, change of mood, and aggressive impulsiveness, for example, have strong inherited components. Another behavior sometimes displayed in the absence of limits, a search of excitement— which corresponds to the desire for passion and sometimes to the danger of being bored — is also correlated with other BPD parameters, such as impulsiveness and violence. The Interesting thing is that some researches have associated this observable behavior with chemical dysregulation of the system of serotonin neurotransmitters and other studies on a specific human chromosome with a gene loci involving a dopamine neurotransmitter. Though true, these studies suggest links between biology, internal chemical equilibrium, and ultimately behavior.

Family studies have shown that first-grade borderline relatives are five times more likely to diagnose the BPD as the public. Borderline family members are also more likely to be diagnosed with related diseases, especially with drug abuse, affective disorders, and anti-social personality disorder. During one's life, specific genes have been affected, in a way, "on and off," by factors such as parental status. Positive parenting can impact genetic predisposition and subsequent biochemical equilibrium in animal and human research that tests maternal care. A person may thus be born with indigenous vulnerabilities to impaired brain circuitry to modulate moods and impulsivity. Still, environmental factors may influence gene expression to determine whether or not the person has any or all potential limited symptoms. Undoubtedly, genetic contributions to the development of BPD — altered by environmental influences — are dependent on several factors and likely involve several chromosomal loci. Nonetheless, further clarification of these processes will perhaps lead to the development of new biotech medicines that can target specific adaptation gene.

Chapter 7: Psychotherapy

Research on bipolar disorder shows that patient who takes medications combine with therapy are more likely to get better faster and avoid relapse. Therapy can teach you how to deal with problems your symptoms are causing, including self-esteem issues, relationship, and work. Therapy also addresses any other problem you are facing, such as anxiety or substance abuse.

Trained mental health professionals can:

Reduce the severity of the attack by intervening early in manic and depressive episodes.

Monitor the patient's on-going status

Help comply with drug regimes

Teach patients to recognize and manage early warning symptoms of imminent depressive or manic episodes.

Educate patients about the illness and its treatment.

In addition, psychotherapy can also help patients:

Deal with feelings of imperfection and despair

Cope with feelings of guilt and remorse that happen after manic episodes

Adjust to the reality of the illness and understand the adverse effects of mania, especially important for patients who consider their mania to be creative, exhilarating and positive.

Cognitive-Behavioral Therapy

Therapists trained in CBT or cognitive-behavioral therapy may be particularly helpful for many patients. CBT is a well-structured, conscious technique that helps the patient understand negative thoughts and behavioral patterns and how to alter them. CBT is also helpful for other mood disorders, including anxiety and depression. Some studies suggest that it if extremely beneficial for bipolar patients. For bipolar disorder patients, CBT aims to:

Identify manic episodes before they become severe and change behaviors during an attack.

Fight depression by developing thoughts and behaviors that may help offset the negative mood.

Family Therapy

For bipolar patients, it is important that their parents, family members or both be involved in therapy. Therapy can help them learn how to deal with bipolar conditions, the need for medications, how to handle the patients during an episode. Recommendations for supporting the patient include:

As a first step, create a treatment contract. In this contract, the patient and family must agree to certain steps, including requests for hospitalization.

Bipolar disorder is dissimilar to alcoholism. So family members of the bipolar patient must be strongly supportive because of the suicidal tendency of the patient. Being empathic and listening attentively can help.

Encourage the patient to comply with treatment. Including force hospitalization, if the patient fails to comply.

Always ready to contract the psychiatrist authorized to treat the patient.

Family members shouldn't feel guilty and shouldn't make the patient feel guilty.

Bipolar disorder can affect the family members of the patient too. Family members should learn to care for themselves and lower the stress and anxiety that accompanies the illness. Internet message boards and support groups can be very helpful for caregivers.

Interpersonal and Social Rhythm Therapy

This type of therapy helps reduces stress in the patient's life and because stress is a trigger for bipolar disorder, this relationship-centered approach can help lower mood cycling. Interpersonal therapy focuses on current relationship issues and helps the patient improve the way they relate to the important people in their life.

IPSRT focuses on maintaining a regular schedule of daily activities to lower likely triggers and improve patients' emotional stability. With IPSRT, patients also learn to avoid problems with personal relationships. Initial evidence indicates that IPSRT combined with medication may help prevent new manic episodes.

Chapter 8: What Are The Causes And Risk Factors For Bipolar Disorder?

The exact cause of bipolar disorder remains to be a mystery. Scientists are still searching for the possible reasons behind it. Most argue that it is caused by multiple factors possibly linked with each other producing the disorder itself or conditions that increase the risk. These factors involve genetic, environmental and neurochemical factors that probably interact on many levels playing a crucial role in the onset and development of bipolar disorder.

Genetic factors

Bipolar disorder tends to be inherited. Current statistics shows that about half of individuals diagnosed with bipolar disorder have a blood relative (e.g. parent, sibling) who also has a mental condition such as obsessive-compulsive disorder (OCD) and depression. This knowledge prompted researchers to look for certain genes that increase one's chance to develop bipolar disorder. Genes function as helpers; it helps in controlling how the human mind and body works. These are integral part of heredity encoded inside an individual's cells and are continuously passed down from parents to their children.

Statistics:

Studies reveal that an individual who has a parent with bipolar disorder has a 15 to 25% chance of having the same mental problem.

A person with a fraternal twin diagnosed with this illness has a 25% chance of having the same condition.

An individual who has an identical twin with bipolar disorder has an even greater risk of developing the same condition as identical twins shares the same exact genetic material. This increases the risk of about eight times as compared to those with non-identical twins.

Environmental factors

Other than genetic factors, scientists believe that other risk factors may increase the development of bipolar disorder. Recent identical twin studies have shown that not all twin of a person with this condition develops bipolar disorder. This finding suggests that other factors besides genes are at play. This would now involve the environment. Certain traits were observed including:

☐Drug/alcohol abuse, bad habits and even hormonal problems trigger manic or depressive episodes even to individuals without family history of bipolar disorder.

Life events such as abuse, stress, trauma or death of a loved one triggers extreme mood swings on a person with a family history of bipolar disorder.

First symptoms of bipolar disorder are increasingly occurring at early age. This change is argued as a result of varying environmental and social factors that are yet to be understood.

Substance abuse worsens bipolar disorder during the recovery period. Tranquilizers and alcohol may trigger severe depression.

Neurochemical factors

Imbalance on certain brain chemicals known as neurotransmitters appears to play a critical role in mood problems particularly in bipolar disorder. Neurotransmitters are chemical messengers involving serotonin, norepinephrine and many others causing this biological disorder. Bipolar disorder may lie dormant for years and may be triggered on its own or by environmental factors such as social problems and psychological stress.

Are there any illnesses/health conditions that can co-occur with bipolar disorder?

Other illnesses may co-exist with bipolar disorder. Determining the presence of these comorbidities is important in preventing undesirable consequences. One of the most common conditions that exist together with bipolar disorder is substance abuse. Adults and teenagers diagnosed with bipolar disorder are at a very high risk of developing alcohol and/or drug abuse. This happens as some people resort to drinking binges and drug use to treat their symptoms. It is important however to note that substance abuse can prolong recovery and may even trigger manic or depressive episodes.

Another condition that may co-exist with bipolar disorder includes attention deficit hyperactivity disorder (ADHD). ADHD often occurs on individuals who have had presented bipolar symptoms during their childhood. People, particularly children with bipolar disorder and ADHD at the same time manifest difficulty in concentrating and controlling their actions. These are evident even when they are not experiencing the typical mood swings seen on bipolar disorder.

Anxiety disorders including generalized anxiety disorder, separation anxiety, social phobia and post-traumatic stress disorder (PTSD) often co-exist with bipolar disorder. This may occur in adults and children alike. Individuals diagnosed with bipolar disorder are also placed at a higher risk of developing heart problems, migraine, diabetes, obesity and other physical illnesses.

Diagnosing and treating bipolar disorder becomes complicated with the presence of these illnesses. Hence, it is critical for individuals suspected of having bipolar disorder to monitor their mental as well as their physical health. Changes and improvements experienced upon treatment should be immediately reported.

How does bipolar disorder affect my life or someone who has it?

Bipolar disorder is an illness that typically lasts in a lifetime. Manic and depressive episodes recur without treatment. However, many continue to manifest symptoms even after receiving appropriate and continuous treatment.

The following are the types of bipolar disorder:

Bipolar I disorder

Bipolar 1 disorder is characterized by mixed episodes of mania and depression that lasts for at least a week. It is also defined by severe manic symptoms requiring prompt hospital care. Manic and depressive episodes in this type of bipolar disorder should be identified as an abnormal behavior disrupting one's life.

Bipolar II disorder

Bipolar II disorder on the other hand is characterized by mood shifting between hypomanic and depressive episodes. The manic episodes however in this type of bipolar disorder do not reach full-blown mixed or manic episodes.

Cyclothymia

Cyclothymia is considered as a mild form of bipolar disorder. Individuals diagnosed with it experiences episodes of hypomania that may shift to mild depression and are not as long-lasting or chronic as that of full depression.

Mixed bipolar

Mixed bipolar is characterized by episodes involving both the symptoms of full blown manic and depressive episodes. Individuals experiencing this type of bipolar disorder are moody, angry, anxious and typically apprehensive. They also experience grandiose and racing thoughts.

Rapid cycling bipolar disorder

This type of bipolar disorder is characterized by rapid mood shifting for about four or more episodes occurring within a year. These periods should last for a few days to consider it as distinct episodes. Rapid cycling may occur anytime during the illness course but experts believe that it occurs at the later stages of life. Women are said to be affected by rapid cycling bipolar disorder more often than men. This rapid cycling pattern increases suicidal risk and severe depression. Use of anti-depressants as a treatment method is thought to elicit and prolong rapid cycling episodes.

Bipolar disorder gets worse without appropriate and timely treatment. Individuals who have it experience more severe and recurrent periods as compared to when its symptoms initially appeared. Delays in correctly identifying it as bipolar disorder can make patients experience troubles on job/school performance. It significantly affects one's ability to perform school activities and hold a job. It also affects one's social as well as personal life. Therefore, it is critical that proper diagnosis and timely treatment is achieved to help people with bipolar disorder lead healthy and productive lives. This will further help in reducing the frequency and severity of its manifestations.

Chapter 9: Causes Of Bipolar Disorder

There is no exact cause of bipolar disorder. However, there are various factors that can trigger this condition. As such, it is essential for people to know these triggering factors that result to bipolar episodes. These include the following:

Neurotransmitters: If there is an imbalance in the brain, this can also result to mood swings and bipolar disorder. Neurotransmitters are brain chemicals that can occur naturally in the brain.

Hormones: If you have hormonal imbalance, this can also be one of the known triggering causes for bipolar disorder. Your hormones affect your moods.

Environmental Factors: Various environmental factors that affect us everyday can also result to bipolar episodes. Factors like stress, traumatic incidents, abuse, etc. are all contributing factors.

Genes: Just like in any other medical condition, bipolar disorder can also be attributed to genes. If you happen to have a family member who also has this disorder, chances are you might also have it especially if it is combined with other factors that trigger bipolar disorder.

Risk Factors of Bipolar Disorder

On top of the known causes for this condition, there are also factors that can increase the risk of developing bipolar disorder like the following:

Long periods of stress

Major changes in life and traumatic incidences

Alcohol and Drug abuse

Parents or siblings with bipolar disorder

Individuals in their early 20s are also at risk of having bipolar disorder

Chapter 10: Is Trust Possible?

When we enter any relationship we bring with us a personal history that informs and influences our expectations of trust in that relationship. Hopefully, as our new relationship unfolds we develop a growing trust, one based on an increased sense of an emotional alliance and dependability. Yet, there are times when a partner may disappoint us, based either on our own misperceptions or by genuinely not living up to our expectations. So, what about someone who has a mental condition that may compel him to do things he may not normally do? Can you trust your bipolar partner? For that matter, can he trust you, given that you may have to report his behavior if it grows extreme? The fact that bipolar people sometimes suffer paranoid delusions may also undermine your partner's trust in you. While issues regarding trust are a part of every relationship, loving someone with bipolar illness brings with it unique concerns for both establishing and maintaining trust.

All Relationships Have Trust Issues

No one ever fully knows another person. Even couples married for fifty years have things they have never told each other. And it is not necessarily because they are ashamed or deceitful. It can simply be because the human memory is faulty or that we sometimes have a very biased version of events. It can also be because we simply don't think something is worth mentioning or that mentioning it will lead to unnecessary complications.

ASK THE DOCTOR

How important is honesty?

If you feel that communication between you and your partner is not good, you may want to consider how much and how well you communicate rather than placing the blame entirely on the other person. In general, bipolar people love to talk, so what you may need is more experience or training in helping to guide the conversation in meaningful ways.

Sharing personal information about ourselves or keeping secrets is one of the major ways we determine what type of relationship we will have with other people. It is a way to measure or express how much we care about them. We want Person A to know something but not Person B, because we like and trust Person A more. There would be no coupling or best friendships if we could not make our own choices about how much to share with whom. Besides, we need to know that our lives and the decisions we make, for better or worse, ultimately belong to us and not somebody else. What to share and with whom are our choices to make. Additionally, the capacity to not have to share everything reflects an ability to comfortably live within one's own skin. It reflects to some degree a healthy relationship with oneself that does not always need an audience, validation, or advice regarding daily decisions and challenges.

Even when we do share something, we keep in mind how much to share and how to share such information; how you describe an incident to your best friend may be different from how you describe it to your mother-in-law. We also talk about our version of events. Sometimes we're willing to admit we're wrong or that whatever happened was at least partially our fault — particularly, when the topic in question happened some time ago. But most of the time, when we talk about ourselves and what we've done, we tend to make ourselves out to be the "good guy." Many people have a difficult time admitting personal faults and often attempt to "save face" regarding how others perceive them — and how they perceive themselves.

Imperfect beings that we are, sometimes we do things that we want to conceal from our partners. Sometimes decent and honest people fib to their partner about when they paid a bill, how the car got dented, or whether they gave Junior a candy bar when he was not supposed to have one. Whereas we might appear accepting and forgiving of such minor transgressions, these little "white lies" may help us preserve our sense of self — an identity more comfortable to live with than that exposed under full disclosure.

You may draw some comfort in acknowledging that "mini" secrets are common to all relationships and that loving someone bipolar is not unique in this respect. Trust issues have little to do with the fact that you have a bipolar partner, but if his symptoms are amplifying, other considerations should be kept in mind.

Learn to Recognize Acting-Out

Let's revisit the major bipolar symptoms: on a basic level, is your partner seeming to lapse into depression and/or mania? Does he seem indifferent? Is it impossible for her to sit still? Is he eating and sleeping? Does she not want to talk? Is he speaking nonstop and very rapidly? Remember that these sudden behavioral changes may signal an impending episode. These behaviors may similarly suggest that your partner is experiencing some form of stress that has triggered her symptoms. Be mindful that she may be concealing alcohol abuse, her negligence in following a medication regimen, or even an insufficient sleep pattern. If any of these signals are apparent, start looking deeper. At such moments it may be helpful to trust your distrust rather than ignore or minimize it.

Money Issues

Seemingly out of nowhere, a person can make unwise investments or business decisions during a manic phase. He may elect to buy everyone in the bar an expensive bottle of champagne or impulsively fly out of town to go gambling. Your partner may even decide to give a large sum of money to a best friend, a relative, or to some worthy cause. Since mania involves an inflated sense of self, it can naturally lead to compulsive spending.

WORD TO THE WISE

Avoid the Use of Money as Medication

Many people take pleasure in the "plastic cure" when unhappy or worried, as if the ability to charge anything they want — even if unaffordable — will make them feel better. They don't realize their high is temporary and will end abruptly with their next credit card bill.

The high that comes with compulsive spending is similar to what an alcoholic feels when she reaches for a bottle. The person who feels invisible may reach for the credit card as a way to convince herself that she deserves whatever she can get and no one should stand in her way. Spending can be a self-soothing strategy, an approach that confirms the feeling of being at least "okay," if not better than others. That part of the self that would normally say "slow down, you're wrecking your life" is not functioning during a manic attack.

At other times your partner may not spend money but will create other emotional challenges by how he manages money. For example, he may feel paranoid enough to withdraw all your shared savings to keep the money "safe" at home. Deceit regarding money undermines trust and, in the extreme, conflicts over money can end a relationship. Adults want to feel a sense of financial autonomy. To be denied access to household resources is humiliating and can make an adult feel as though he's being treated like a child. The resulting feeling of inequality is a motivating force for a bipolar partner to keep secrets from his mate.

Monitoring Money

If you know your partner has a history of spending problems and her symptoms are out of control, you may need to understand the details of her binging to maintain a trusting relationship.

For starters, try monitoring your account balances online. If some accounts are more difficult to access, consider converting them to a more accessible and secure venue. If your partner is manic and some of your money is unaccounted for, you need to set boundaries.

If your partner has a history of money issues driven by mania, work out a system to minimize a reoccurrence. Perhaps you want a joint account but also private accounts for both you and your partner so you can save or spend as you choose. The joint account (or investments) can be set up to require both signatures. You can also speak confidentially with a banker or an accountant about additional strategies. If your partner still finds a way around these security measures, it may be time for tough love and a new approach so the only money your partner receives is what you give her. Should your partner complain, be firm. Explain that if the relationship is to continue, the plan is not negotiable. You may want to find other things that your partner can take responsibility for, like landscaping the yard or selecting a new refrigerator, while you handle the finances. Although this approach may at times feel uncomfortable, know that you are protecting both of you from a potentially damaging outcome.

If you are engaged in a serious conversation — possibly in a professional setting — money issues should be part of that discussion. Some people neglect to discuss money, especially in a conversation of some depth, but if you are hurt, angry, and frustrated when the budget falls apart, you can — and should — express those thoughts. You may even mention your sadness, anxiety, and disappointment when compulsive overspending diminishes your shared potential to enjoy a more rewarding life. More importantly, your partner's impulsive choices can create financial debt that both of you may carry for many years. Most significant, you need to underscore how binge spending undermines your trust in your partner and your relationship.

Work Issues

While some bipolar sufferers can successfully hold a job, others cannot. Even if highly successful, there may be periods where your partner is unable to work because of his bipolar symptoms. If you're not independently wealthy, this sudden departure from work can be a significant, long-term loss of household income.

This also means your partner will be spending more time at home. Although this can be nice, it can potentially lead to further conflict and problems. When there is less order in your partner's life, he may fill the void with unconstructive activities. Any lack of structure coupled with mania can lead to extra purchases that could add to your financial difficulties.

Frequently, someone who is unemployed for a period of time begins to enjoy her idle status. After being discouraged by repeated rejections when seeking new employment, people prone to depression are likely to feel that they need a few days, a week, or even a month to recover from their disappointment. At such moments, your partner may conclude that she has not made progress, or that her disorder will prevent her from succeeding in the future. This is a time when your love and affection is most needed, and a little TLC can go a long way. Your partner may also benefit from talking to an employment counselor about how to handle job interviews. It's beneficial to schedule this appointment as soon as possible — even the same day — since mania can lead to very unfocused behavior and a million other things might stand in the way of your partner keeping a scheduled appointment. With a little humor, you can encourage your partner to seek help now rather than later — other things can wait, and "later" can be never.

WORD TO THE WISE

Create an Advanced Directive

One of the most important things you can do in a bipolar relationship is to create an advance directive. This is a signed legal document in which your bipolar partner gives permission for another individual (such as a doctor or family member) to ensure that she receives proper treatment — even hospitalization — should she experience another episode.

At the same time, let her know that your trust depends more on what she does to help herself and the relationship than on whether she maintains a specific job.

Violent Impulses

During severe manic episodes, a bipolar individual may become very harmful to himself or others. This may involve violence up to and including murder or suicide. If a manic person feels seriously threatened, there may be an eruption of violent behavior. By contrast, the desire to escape the intense anxiety and agitation that may accompany these episodes is often a major aspect of the motivation for suicide.

Even if murder or suicide is not the outcome, a bipolar person can seriously harm herself through reckless mania or a botched suicide attempt. Likewise, she can bring injury to others by causing a serious accident or expressing anger through physical violence. It's understandable that the unpredictability of behavior during such episodes may greatly undermine your capacity to trust your partner.

If your partner gets violent, you should leave immediately. Don't assume you can calm your partner down. If you must sneak out or make up some excuse to leave, do whatever is necessary to stay safe. If you have children, take them with you. If you have a cell phone, enter 911 and the local police department number into your speed dial. You may also want to put a close friend or a family member on speed dial. Ideally, this should be someone who can manage an emergency. Remember, no one deserves an abusive relationship, and physical assault of another person is against the law. Unfortunately, there is no guarantee that the violence will stop.

Can I Believe What My Partner Says?

Even in less dramatic scenarios, your manic partner may demonstrate behaviors that make you wonder how much you can trust her. She may, for example, burst into a talking marathon chatting about anything and everything. Sometimes the chatter digresses into rhyming or stoned-like incoherence, but even before this happens you may wonder if your partner is being truthful or just talking to talk. This can mean that your partner is telling possible untruths about actual situations, opinions, and attitudes. For example, she is a Democrat, but she gets into a long-drawn-out discussion with a Republican and suddenly claims to be Republican. Depression can compel people to say many things they would never say if not depressed: "Life is hopeless," "Nobody cares about me," and so on.

WORD TO THE WISE

No Guns Allowed

If your bipolar partner is interested in guns or other weapons, even for display purposes, it's wise to insist he take up a different hobby. Be honest. Say that you worry about guns in the house and that he should do this for you.

Since manic behaviors may leave you disoriented and questioning what really is true, it may be wise to accept your partner's talking marathons with a grain of salt. Many of us exaggerate at times or agree just for the sake of agreeing, but depression distorts reality in a different way. When things are calm, your bipolar partner is not necessarily any more honest or dishonest than the next person.

Setting Adult Boundaries

Part of being an adult is accepting who you are and determining guidelines and structure for how you want to live your life. Simultaneously, a loving relationship requires realistic compromises based on trust and candid communication. You can always ask your partner if he wants to behave in a certain way that may be more consistent with your expectation of how a relationship should be. Similarly, he is free to decide and to compromise if he chooses to do so. However, you cannot will your partner's bipolar disorder away, nor can you control the effectiveness of his treatment. But, you can choose to accept these realities and work things out accordingly.

Case Study: Rick and Susan

Conflicts surrounding control issues can surface in any relationship. And when they do occur, they can greatly impact the level of trust between partners. Certain dynamics in a bipolar relationship may make both of you vulnerable to having such conflicts. This is what transpired for Rick, age thirty-eight, and Susan, thirty-two.

Rick was diagnosed with bipolar disorder during the second year of their six-year relationship. This diagnosis immediately moved Susan into a familiar situation, as she had played a very active and involved role in caring for her mother, who had a history of depression. From early adolescence on, often to the neglect of her own needs, Susan devoted much of her time and concern with her mother. For this reason, she felt very prepared to focus all of her energies on helping Rick to manage his illness. However, although well intended, Susan's intense vigilance regarding Rick's well-being and her detailed attention to his behavior gradually left him feeling treated like a child. He brought to the relationship his own sensitivity to feeling controlled, as he had grown up with a mother who was overly intrusive and minimally respected his boundaries. This left him, at times, prone to self-doubt and, in part, more vulnerable to not feeling independent. Subsequently, Rick had a predisposition to perceive Susan as being more like a parent than a loving partner.

Rick's resentment increased in the two years following his diagnosis. Rather than discuss his reactions, he would become irritable and at times explosive. In an attempt to experience greater control over his life, he became increasingly less communicative and isolated himself. His withdrawal fostered Susan's anxiety and distrust, which only increased her desire to be vigilant.

While Susan acted from her deep love for her partner, she had unwittingly behaved in ways that actually left Rick feeling abandoned, desiring a loving partner, and feeling more like she was a parent. The dynamics of their interactions led to a breakdown in trust and much turmoil that impaired effective communications. It was only after Rick's repeated episodes of anger that he and Ann both sought counseling to help them understand how their interactions undermined their mutual trust.

Tough Love

If you want a teenager to think you are cool and a "best friend," you can sit back and let him have complete say about whether or not he attends school, uses drugs, or what time he returns home at night. Or, you can risk having him get angry with you — even temporarily hate you — by insisting he stay in school, telling him that he must have a curfew, and that under no circumstances is he to use drugs. Similarly, if your mate is starting to show signs of mania or depression, you can sit back and let it happen to avoid having conflict and anger directed toward you. Or, for the good of your partner and all concerned, you can take one or all of the following actions:

· **Call the doctor.** If your partner is seeing a doctor, call her and report that various symptoms seem to be acting up.

· **Call a family member or friend.** Let someone you trust know what is happening. If things get truly bad, you (and your children) should have a place you can go temporarily.

· **Check around the house.** No one likes to feel spied on, and people who snoop around usually feel guilty or afraid of getting caught. Still, carefully looking things over can be in the best interest of you and your partner. For example, are there unfamiliar folders about business ventures or vacations? Are there unfamiliar names with telephone numbers? Are there objects that could be used to cause harm?

· **Check medication adherence.** Is your partner taking her medication? Taking too much medication? Has your partner introduced another medication or herbal supplement? These suggestions are not intended to make you overly anxious or hypervigilant, but rather to alert you to areas of concern.

· **Look for changes in routines.** If your partner works outside the home, has he been going to work? Has he shown changes in the time he goes to bed or wakes up? Has he abruptly stopped an exercise regimen that he has been following? Has there been a change in your partner's social contacts?

· **Talk to your partner.** Explain that some recent behaviors appear symptomatic of an episode. Make it clear that you're not passing judgment, but that you have noticed (for example) that she has not eaten in twenty-four hours and that you're concerned and want to accompany her to the doctor or do whatever it takes to help.

Learning from Mistakes

Since no relationship is perfect, frequently a couple's best approach is to learn from past mistakes. While some partners never get past the stage of mistrust, others manage to stay together. Re-establishing trust requires a shared acceptance that the problem is abating or has been eliminated.

Talk It Over

When your partner has calmed down, take this opportunity to talk about what happened in a nonconfrontational tone. When you have arrived at some understanding, you can mutually decide how things can be improved in the future. Couples counseling is recommended, but even if you're seeing a therapist the two of you need to make time to talk together.

ASK THE DOCTOR

How can I manage conflict?

One effective guideline to help couples manage conflict is to agree in advance on a key word that can be used as a signal to drop a contentious subject during a heated discussion. For example, choose whimsical words such as "cheese ball," "monkey," or "jelly bean." Either partner can use the key signal with the understanding that the issue will be discussed at a later time when you have both cooled off. While this tactic will not work if your partner is severely manic, it can be useful at other times.

One of your big surprises might be the discovery of how your partner feels. When one partner assumes responsibility for the stability of the relationship, there is the tendency to forget about the other person's needs and feelings. Helping someone does not guarantee their gratitude. Even with the best of intentions, your partner may feel resentful about her dependent role and inability to contribute. Eventually, the dependent partner will begin to feel infantilized. Feeling treated like a child leads to resentment and the need to act out, a way of regaining some sense of independence and "equal" adult status.

Keep in mind that people who seem to enjoy or to expect others to wait on them want to also have the choice of acting independently. While most of us enjoy occasional pampering, few are comfortable being overindulged. Do not assume that your partner should be shielded from all frustration because of his bipolar illness. While too much stress can be overwhelming, learning to effectively manage frustration fosters a sense of mastery and self-confidence. Although you may, at times, distrust that your partner can manage frustration on her own, being in tune with her history will help you feel fortified and accepting of this challenge.

WORD TO THE WISE

Use Compassion

Remember, when your partner is acting out his illness, it's not intentional. Conversely, if you lose patience with your partner and purposefully make her feel badly, you're acting without compassion. When intentionally inflicting pain, you may be reacting from your own discomfort. Your hurt needs to be addressed, and you'll neither help yourself nor your relationship by causing your partner pain.

Be aware of your motives when communicating with your partner.

It's essential that you're aware of these tendencies and that you and your partner discuss the challenges as they occur. Conversations of this nature may be difficult to begin, but if the issues are ignored your partner may start acting out her feelings rather than discussing them. Talking things out can lead to self-discovery for both of you. Your partner might find better ways of articulating what his symptoms feel like, and you can be more in touch with your own feelings and needs by expressing them.

Protection Can Mean Love

While being attentive to how you impact the relationship, there may be times when you need to change the name on an account, add or change the locks, or enforce new rules. By approaching delicate matters in a loving way, your partner won't feel like you are treating him like a child. You can convey your intentions of keeping everyone safe and happy by heeding the new regimen. Try to address these security concerns in a collaborative manner. For example, if your partner acknowledges that he is in agreement about his not having access to important documents, this allows you to begin a discussion of alternative strategies for their safekeeping.

You may also point out that you still feel loved and protected by your partner in many different ways. Besides protecting your finances, the trust you have in your partner may depend on him taking proper care of himself. Sometimes you may need to play an active role in ensuring that he does so. For example, firmly communicate that while you understand your partner is feeling angry or depressed, you will not listen to him until he has something to eat. You may even need to abide by a strictly observed bedtime. Any of these guidelines can be done in a manner that conveys genuine love and concern rather than a harsh tone that sounds like a demand for obedience.

Do Not Be a Scapegoat

Occasionally you may even blame yourself for your partner's behavior. For example, you may recall having supported his request for one more beer at a party when you might have prevented his indulgence. Or, maybe because of your desire to enjoy an evening with friends, you convinced your partner to stay out later than usual. If your partner tries to blame you for his resulting mania or depression, don't let yourself become a scapegoat and berate yourself with guilt. Remember, even if you did contribute to his mood change, it is his illness that makes him vulnerable. Learn from your actions and be more mindful in the future.

You may also be blamed for your partner's reactions even when you did nothing to trigger them. At such moments, always remember the true nature of bipolar disorder. If he accuses you of placing the responsibility on him for his own symptoms, let your partner know that the blame game is not the point. If there is any possibility that he might be right, apologize while reminding him that the goal is not to point fingers but rather figure out a solution. Always keep the tone on an adult level.

ASK THE DOCTOR

What are some positive aspects about living with a bipolar partner?

One potentially positive aspect of living with a bipolar person who acts out from time to time is to learn an important lesson about what to take personally and what to let go. This is especially true if you tend to have your own "trigger points" that make you sensitive to criticism. Though challenging, you need to remember that it is your partner's illness talking and go about your business, even if what was said about you was not nice.

Your partner may even be camouflaging her own sense of guilt and embarrassment by lashing out at you. This may not be fair, but it's about your partner's inability to cope; it is not about you. It might be comforting to remind yourself of this, while simultaneously reminding your partner that everyone messes up at times. Nobody is perfect. It is through such compassionate communication that you can experience a sense of alliance with each other and achieve mutual trust.

What Can You Do Differently?

Once the crisis has passed, take an inventory of yourself. Have you made mistakes? For example:

· Did you yell at your kids, friends, or coworkers because of your frustration with your partner? If so, apologize and deal with your own stress issues. Talk to a professional if you believe it will help.

· Did you neglect your own needs and responsibilities? Did you end up not eating or sleeping? Did you have to miss work?

· Do you have unrealistic expectations for your partner, given the relative severity of his condition? If your bipolar partner realistically cannot work outside the home, you need to decide if you can accept and live with this decision. By contrast, if you harbor completely unrealistic expectations of what you would like your partner to become, release them, because all they are doing is hurting you, your partner, and your relationship.

· Do you still love your partner? This is a tough one. You may feel guilty if the answer is "no," because you don't want to hurt him or you feel that he "needs" you. You may even feel it is a sign of weakness or selfishness on your part to value concerns like financial stability over caring for another person.

Remember, trust in any relationship involves being candid with each other whether the goal is to promote a growing relationship or to end one. While the latter outcome can be painful, it is much better for both individuals when the subject is discussed with honesty and compassion. It also is a more mature and responsible alternative to the conflict and the turmoil that may otherwise arise when the real issues are not confronted.

Chapter 11: Causes Or Risk Factors

No known causes of bipolar disorder have been discovered, and researchers are yet to discover the specific genes that contribute to the disorder or understand the manner of physical changes that occur in the brain when the disorder is present. However, researchers have a sense of the factors that heighten your chances of developing the disorder. Having a family member with the condition significantly increases the risk due to its highly heritable nature. Although some people are genetically predisposed to the risk of the disorder, not all of them eventually develop bipolar disorder. This goes to suggest that psychological factors and environmental factors can trigger manic or depressive episodes, but not everyone suffering from the disorder will experience these episodes.

Family with the Disorder

Having a relative that has bipolar disorder in your nuclear family, such as a parent or sibling, places you at an increased risk for the disorder. Symptoms may initially show up during teenage years or early adulthood, with an average onset being 25 years. An analysis of the literature discovered that children whose parents have a severe mental illness had roughly a one-third chance of becoming mentally ill by adulthood. Researchers have also discovered that if a parent is diagnosed with the disorder at an early age, the child has a higher risk for also developing it.

However, genetics isn't the only factor. Studies conducted on identical twins have revealed that although bipolar disorder is highly heritable, both twins will not necessarily develop the disorder, which means that environmental factors can also play a role in increasing or reducing the risk of having the disorder.

High Stress

People who undergo traumatic events have a higher risk of developing bipolar disorder. Childhood factors like neglect, sexual or physical abuse, the loss of a parent, or other traumatic events can heighten the chances of developing the disorder later in life. Extremely stressful events like moving to a new environment, losing a job, or a death in the family can also trigger manic or depressive episodes. Little or no sleep can also increase the risk of a manic episode.

Substance Abuse

Abuse of drugs or alcohol can also increase the risk of developing bipolar disorder. The use of substance doesn't directly cause the disorder, but it can worsen mood episodes or hasten the onset. Medications also have the ability to trigger the onset of a manic or depressive episode. However, you may have to detox from substances before a doctor can diagnose bipolar disorder due to the fact that substance use can trigger psychosis.

Brain Structure

Two types of scans that can take images of the brain are functional magnetic resonance imaging (fMRI) and positron emission technology (PET). Certain findings on brain scans may be linked to bipolar disorder but more research is required to determine how these findings specifically impact bipolar disorder and how this affects treatment and diagnosis.

Gender

Bipolar disorder affects men and women in equal parts, but women are three times more at risk to undergo rapid cycling of mood episodes. Compared to men, women are also more at risk of experiencing depressive and mixed episodes of the disorder. To determine whether you're at risk for bipolar disorder, you can ask the following questions:

Is anyone in your family suffering from bipolar disorder or another mental illness?

Have you experienced any form of trauma in your childhood?

Did you undergo recent stressful events or lack of sleep?

Have you observed extreme changes in your mood after using drugs or alcohol?

Have these extreme mood changes affected your work, daily activities, or relationships?

Even if your answer to these questions is "no," you can still consult your doctor or a mental health professional about your concerns so as to receive a diagnostic evaluation. If you already have the disorder and are worried about the risks of your own children, talk to a professional to help you determine the interventions that can help them maintain good mental wellness.

Chapter 12: The Principles Of Cbt

Cognitive Behavioral Therapy (CBT) is usually suggested as part of a complete treatment plan for bipolar. It works by affecting the mood swings and leveling out the extremes. The treatment capitalizes on connecting thoughts and emotions to physical actions so that you can interrupt your damaging thoughts. The method teaches you to identify your negative thought patterns, much like positive thinking, only instead of simply turning your thoughts around you respond in a less drastic way. It's a step that can help you if you're struggling with positive thinking methods.

How does it work?

CBT is a form of cognitive restructuring. It basically helps you change your thinking and correct problems. It's usually taught through therapy where you learn to recognize and catch distortions and overblown thoughts and know that they come from your disease and not from reality. It's a good way of preventing major changes before they happen. It's a form of problem solving that gives you a chance to recognize the problem with your thoughts, think of a solution, and then create a reasonable outcome without panicking. It can be applied to any part of life where stress occurs and may cause a lapse.

What is it?

CBT acts as a selection of techniques together to make your daily life function better and be more stable. The first step to using CBT is accepting your diagnosis. Many people avoid the stigma of mental health problems by simply denying that they are there, but it's been proven that the brain of patients is physically different so this is not only unfair but useless. Embracing the diagnosis makes the concept of reaching out and getting help much easier. By reaching out you're also able to access much of the support that exists around you such as in religious communities, social activities, and professional help. It can also help you by making you more aware of your symptoms and triggers so that you can better avoid them or tackle them when they appear.

Monitoring

Part of CBT is monitoring yourself. Bipolar is an especially hard disease to treat because the symptoms are so changeable. On a daily basis, you may swing wildly or you may not change for days at a time. Being aware of your thoughts and your actions and noting them down can help professionals better suggest methods for your treatment. Rating your mood daily, noting any particular triggers or changes, and even noting any calming actions as well as the response to medication is part of a successful treatment plan.

Part of monitoring yourself also means that you'll learn to recognize your triggers and warnings so you can avoid them. Common triggers are usually stress related and can include financial issues, arguments, school and work issues, lack of sleep, and even seasonal changes. Both mania and depression have distinct red flags when relapse is occurring so it's important to note these symptoms too so you can head them off.

With depression craving chocolate is one of the foremost signs, there's also an excessive need for sleep, a desire for isolation, and a lack of motivation. Mania tends to be characterized by being hungry constantly, feeling energized, not being able to concentrate, and being irritable. Knowing these signs and keeping tabs on them means that they don't get lost in your busy day so the problem spirals. If you can spot the patterns when they arise you can also head them off.

Example Shay:

She's a busy girl, always working but sometimes she just can't force herself to get out of bed. After her diagnosis medication helped but it also let her feeling foggy and would make her take several days a month off feeling sick. In a normal week, her boss would be exceptionally demanding towards the weekends making her feel pressured. When she would get emails from her boss Shay automatically thought she was in trouble and would start panicking. The more she focused on it the more she would worry and over the weekend she would become depressed. On Fridays she would start craving chocolate, and would often leave work early with a huge headache then she would spend Saturday in bed asleep. By monitoring her symptoms she was able to identify that her reaction to her bosses emails were triggering her depressive swing over the weekend and take action to correct her thinking.

Another part of CBT is forming a routine. Having a regular schedule can be a good way to create stability and avoid being triggered by stress. The regular routine allows for proper sleep, meals, social plans, chores and exercise so that you can get both the benefits of alternative therapies and medication while still functioning well. Part of being bipolar is often making excuses during your depressive phase so that you don't do anything, but having a regimented routine you are less likely to deviate and be unproductive which will cause the spiral to continue going down. The routine acts as a checkpoint to stop this.

Maximizing Treatment

CBT only works if you're doing it between therapy sessions. As a technique, you need to practice routine, self-monitoring, and accepting that your diagnosis is true. While changing your thought pattern is hard that is why therapy can help, but you have to make yourself repeat the actions between sessions too. Your actions should be self-regulating and should stop extremes.

Chapter 13: How To Manage Bipolar Disorder

In spite of the fact that there are many ways that one can be able to treat bipolar disorder, the most important thing that we need to recognize is that there is no cure for this kind of mental illness. This means that we only have the ability to manage the illness. The best way to do this is by simply exercising care. The main reason why care is important is the fact that it contributes towards proper diagnosis and acceptance of the illness, it creates an infrastructure that is geared towards providing adequate care and love to the patients, and it definitely contributes towards establishing a better life. The flow chart below indicates how care is achieved and the factors that actively come into play to attain proper lives and normalcy for the persons with bipolar disorder.

When it comes to management, the diagram above indicates the various steps in the journey of managing the disorder with a great degree of success. An important thing to note is that the symptoms of bipolar disorder are often spotted with the manifestation of severe crisis in the life of the person. This is the time when the patient has to go through mandatory treatment according to the Mental Health Act, 2007. However, in the case of people with bipolar disorder type 2 and 3, they have the ability to recognize the onset of the symptoms of their illnesses at a very early stage. This is the time when they are able to consult with their doctors and they can be referred to a psychiatrist for accurate diagnosis.

Lack of Insight

One of the setbacks when it comes to people with bipolar disorder is the fact that they have a distinct lack of insight and destructive behaviors. This, in most cases, for patients with mania often cannot be diagnosed early enough because there is a lack of testing. This means that for an accurate diagnosis to be made, it takes several years.

Towards diagnosis

An important thing to take into consideration as a bipolar patient is accepting the diagnosis outcome. This is because, when you choose to remain in denial, you are simply paving the way for recurrent cycles of crisis and re-diagnosis, if you fail to address this situation, it will last for several years and deteriorate with time and poor health habits

Being a patient with bipolar disorder, I can assure you that it is not easy to accept the fact that you have been diagnosed with this condition. The main reason for this is often the stigma that is associated with most mental illnesses. This is despite the tremendous efforts that many organizations and activists have made in the past few decades. Really, would you want to admit to yourself or anyone else that you are a mental case?

Manic depression is really frightening especially during the early stages. This is because in most cases, you do not have any clue what is happening to you. You often feel that you are out of control and have no idea when this might re-occur. The main reason is that you most likely do not have any control over your emotions and feelings and thus act out of impulse. The result of this is suffering for the people that are closest to you such as family and friends. As I mentioned earlier, it is extremely important that you accept the diagnosis and take control over your life. As someone with the illness, there are three milestones that have helped me cope with my illness and thus, effectively manage my condition despite the various challenges that are faced along the journey. These milestones include;

Acceptance

This is the very first milestone towards managing bipolar disorder. Did you know that illnesses often has the ability to get to the core of your sense of being? Well, this is very true. Mental illness especially has the power to destroy your self-confidence and your self-esteem. This means that if you fail to accept your condition, you are simply marking timing on the same ground and thus, making it much more difficult to move forward. At this very stage, information is very paramount. When you allow yourself to meet people with the similar condition, you are simply allowing them to share their experiences and thus, informing your thought process. Look around your locality, you will not miss a psychiatrist or two who run small groups for people with bipolar disorder. Join them!

Insight

Once you have accepted that you are bipolar, the next step is insight. An episode of their mental illness does not just come out of the blues. The truth of the matter is, almost every person has an alarm warning of some kind of illness. In most cases, these warning signals are often personal. However, if you are experiencing mania, this might manifest through irritability, lack of sleep, intense sexual desires among others. In the case of depression, some of the early signals include tiredness, avoiding the company of people as well as losing interest in pleasurable activities such as sex.

In all this, you have to understand that the occurrence of an episode of bipolar disorder is often triggered by a particular problem. This can be career challenges, personal relationships, and stress among others. In both cases of mania and depression, you have to become aware and vigilant of these changes and ensure that you consult the doctor about any possibilities in changing your medications.

Action

The final milestone is acting. With insight, you will be able to act out of concrete information and evidence rather than acting out blindly. The first thing, in this case, is to come up with an action plan.

This is very critical in ensuring that you have all the practical responses laid out should an episode of bipolar disorder arise. This should be designed in such a way that you can easily follow through whenever you are able to. Additionally, it should have the ability to dictate to the caregivers, family, and close friends, of the effective manner in which they can intervene. Therefore, do not be afraid, rehearse the plan and ensure that you keep it up to date at all times.

Managing your bipolar disorder in an effective manner simply means ensuring that you maintain good mental health between episodes. The best way to achieve this is by ensuring that you keep track of small changes in your mood so that it will be easy for you to determine the early onset of the symptoms. This is very important in ensuring that you can act on it before true depression and mania kicks in. In most cases, mania and depression can be maladaptive responses to aspects of stress. This means that you can use them to ensure that you channel your thoughts somewhere other than problems that you are facing.

When you face problems in life, you develop the ability to sort these problems out and thus, realistically maintain a healthy mental stability. One of the ways in which you can effectively manage bipolar disorder is by ensuring that you perform a regular review of your anxieties and stresses. By doing so, it will enable you to avoid the problems building up and provoking occurrence of a crisis.

In order to achieve this effectively, my advice to you would be to nurture a strong and healthy social network. When you do this, you will soon realize that your close friends, family, and community around you will not be frightened away and thus will serve as valuable tools in giving you helpful feedback to thrust you to the next level of recovery. It is your close relations that will, in most cases, notice that something is not right. Additionally, it is their social support that will go a long way in ensuring that you achieve mental stability and health. Remember, part of staying healthy and whole is taking care of the relationships we have so that we can sail through the turbulence of our illness.

After all, is said and done about managing bipolar disorder, a crucial thing to take note of is that the last two milestones; 'Insight and Action,' have little to do with the treatment of your illness. Rather, it is much more concerned with rebuilding your life once you have adequate mastery and knowledge of the symptoms. It is this knowledge that you have achieved that will not only help you to gain control over potentially damaging impacts of the illness but also help you through the journey towards restoring your self-esteem and confidence.

It is the resulting confidence and self-esteem that will go a long way in helping you to explore novel avenues and life's possibilities. This way, you are simply opening yourself up to new opportunities which will thrust you to new heights that you have always desired and that really is vital to your happiness. You will be surprised at how this plays a critical role in restoring to you; new relationships, interests, security as well as employment/career growth and prosperity.

Stress and Schedule Management

What is the role of stressful situations in Bipolar disorder?

Stressful situations are often triggered by a number of factors. These factors often include things like interpersonal conflicts or financial challenges among others. These factors are attributed to increasing the likelihood of manic and depressive episodes of bipolar disorder. In some cases, life events such as marriage, the pressure at the workplace, shifting jobs among others may be the cause of these episodes. In this chapter, we will discuss the various techniques that you can employ in your treatment. It is important that you select those techniques that you find valuable to improving your condition or that of your loved one.

Managing sleep patterns

Based on research findings, there is a clear indication that alterations in the sleep cycle from normal one often is a trigger to increasing the risks of developing mania of depression. Considering the fact that you cannot always avoid stress, you should ensure that you strive to maintain your normal sleep patterns. The most important thing about this is so that you can be able to maintain a stable mood throughout the day. The best way in which you can employ sleep in buffering against manic and depressive episodes of bipolar disorder is by waking up and retiring to bed at the same time always regardless of whether it is a weekday or a weekend.

Despite the fact that it can be tempting to stay up late or even sleep in during the weekends, any change in your sleep patterns is a recipe for disaster. What I would like you to always remember is that the more consistent you are in the time you wake and go to sleep each day, the more stable your mood will be. You do not have to carry out this strategy in an all-or-nothing manner. Instead, if you find it quite challenging to maintain a regular sleep pattern, it is up to you to select a sleep schedule that is more defined and works best for you especially during stressful periods.

Some of the most important and beneficial sleep tips that you can employ includes the following;

Keeping stress out of the bedroom

When it comes to sleeping, then you should actually exercise sleep. This means that when you get to the bedroom, let it be your number one priority to ensure that you do not discuss any stressful situations concerning your family, job or friends while in the bedroom. Therefore, all you should do is preserve the bedroom for sleep activities only.

Use muscle relaxation techniques while in bed

When you get to bed, you can use relaxation tapes to help enhance your relaxation and thus boost your comfort in bed. Always bear in mind that the goal is not going to sleep. Rather, it is about attaining comfort and relaxation so that sleep is naturally triggered. There are so many commercially available tapes that you can purchase to help you achieve bedtime relaxation.

Do not exert yourself to get to sleep

Whenever you find it difficult to get sleep, refrain from trying too hard! The main reason for this is the fact that when you try too hard to get sleep, you are only causing the opposite effect to take place. This means that you will stay awake and frustrated. The best thing you can do is try to enjoy being in bed and resting. This is irrespective of whether there is sleep or not. First, ensure that you direct your focus on how comfortable you are in bed and the manner in which your muscles are relaxed. In so doing, you are allowing your thoughts to drift slowly into sleep. In other words, you are allowing yourself be passive about sleep and your job is done! This way, sleep will come to you naturally.

Give yourself time to unwind before going to sleep

The best way you can achieve this is by ensuring that the last activity you are doing before going to bed is relatively passive. This means that you do not have to engage in activities that will require so much of your thoughts and trigger stress. Do not try to reflect on your life's problems or plan the week ahead among other unnecessary tasks that can be done gradually or at another time that is more convenient. The best you can do is to save such activities for the time when you feel fresh. Before you go to sleep, you can engage in activities such as; watching television, reading or talking. Unwind and let yourself go to sleep.

Employ a regular daytime cycle to allow you have nighttime sleep

The trick, in this case, is ensuring that you avoid taking naps during the day. Instead, you should employ the use of regular exercise that will induce fatigue and trigger normal sleep during nighttime. Minimize the intake of caffeine, alcohol or cigarette within several hours of retiring to bed. The best way in which you can establish a regular sleep pattern is by ensuring that you have a regular time for getting out of bed. Set your alarm clock to a reasonable time and ensure that you stick to it throughout the entire week. This way, you will be stabilizing your sleep easily.

Adjust sleep cycle prior to traveling

One of the things that have a great potential of disrupting sleep cycle is traveling across time zones, adjust your sleep cycle to match that of the new time zone. However, in cases where your travel is brief, stick to your regular schedule.

Avoid destructive activities

Control over illegal substance abuse

When it comes to things such as drugs and alcohol, these represent a great risk for people suffering from bipolar disorder. This is because, when you ingest these substances, you are impairing the activity of your medications. The main reason is that, when you engage in alcohol and drugs, you simply forget your condition and forget taking medications. This is also associated with increased rate of hospitalization. Particularly, stimulants are known to trigger episodes of mania and depression in people with bipolar disorder. Therefore, it is important that you assess your moods and the condition you are in before you make a decision to take alcohol or drugs.

This is the main reason why most bipolar treatments begin 30 days after one has been clean from drugs and alcohol. If it is about enjoying yourself, there are so many alternative events that you can engage in. Always ensure that you keep your doctor aware of any substances that you are using in the course of the treatment. Remember that you are the core member of your treatment group and thus, it is important that you keep the rest of the team up to date concerning your mood disorder.

How to get an accurate perspective on thoughts

Did you know that thought irrespective of whether they are true or not have a powerful effect on your mood? Well, this is the case and is the reason why it is important to have accurate thoughts. When one is suffering from a mood disorder, the truth is that they often suffer from the accuracy of thoughts. In depressive episodes of bipolar disorder, the thoughts are often negative in nature while in manic episodes, the thoughts are often positive.

It is important to come up with important strategies that will help you to avoid the effect of inaccurate thoughts. The best way in which you can prevent being pushed around by these inaccurate thoughts is treating them as hypotheses or guesses. This means that before you can accept the thought as true, it is important that you assess the thought to determine whether it is helpful or not. How can you assess your thoughts? You can assess your thoughts by ensuring that you look at the presence of evidence for and against each thought you have.

Ensure that you look at what alternative thoughts hold. The truth is that these alternative thoughts may actually have the accurate reflection of the reality. Your thoughts are often an influence of your present mood. Therefore, do not allow your mood to push you around into believing in things that are not accurate. Whenever you have challenges or difficulties in sorting out your thoughts, it might be very useful to discuss your thoughts with people that you trust. This could be a friend or a family member or even your therapist.

Suicidal thinking and self-care

As discussed earlier, it is evident that symptoms of bipolar disorder may include feeling hopeless. This is because when someone is experiencing intense symptoms of the mental illness, they often are very vulnerable to losing hope and feel that life is not worth living. It is these feelings that often slowly strip the mental patient of their sense of self-worth and soon they lose confidence and self-esteem. The consequences of these are, it allows thoughts of harming oneself to creep in and thus suicidal thoughts.

The truth about suicidal thoughts is that they can be frightening and overwhelming in most cases. This often takes place during both depressive and manic episodes of bipolar disorder. One important thing that you have to remember at all times is that suicidal thoughts and alteration of your behavior are all symptoms of bipolar disorder and just like other symptoms, they can be treated. Most of the people who have this illness often seek help and they are supported to get better. The first step, in this case, is for the patient and their family to be aware of the signs of suicide so that they can look out for these.

Some of these warning signs may include; frequent talks about committing suicide or thoughts about death. In other cases, the person might be making concerning comments about being hopeless and worthless indicating that they have lost their self-esteem and confidence and this could potentially pose a great threat to them. Some of the statements that they could be making are; "It would be better if I just died", or "I want out". Other indicators may be that the patient is in a worse situation of depression and experiences sudden changes in their moods. They could voluntarily expose themselves to things that might harm them. Finally, the patient may also be trying to sort their affairs in certain order such as talking about their will, finances and ensuring that all this are patched up in case they die.

If these warning signs are evident, it is important that you take the relevant and necessary steps to protect yourself and your loved ones. The best way you can do this is by simply taking the discussion up with the doctor. You have to understand that suicidal thoughts are symptoms and this is the very reason why you should report this to a mental health professional so that the necessary help can be administered. Based on how severe these thoughts are, it is important during this time, to ensure that you or your loved one accept a brief hospital stay for close monitoring. The purpose of the hospital stay is not to burden you or strip you of your freedom. Instead, it is important in offering you the help, support, and protection that you need until you are feeling better. As a matter of fact, this is the most fundamental and critical aspects of care. A person requires protection during this time of severe symptoms so that they have all the chances and opportunities of improving. I, therefore, want you to take every step necessary to ensure that you are protected and make good use of your treatment team for your own good.

One of the straightforward strategies you can employ is making the process of getting help very easy. This is one of the techniques which have been shown by research to play a significant role in enhancing safety in situations where one has suicidal thoughts. The very step of ensuring that the person has relevant contact information has been demonstrated to play a significant role in protecting individuals from suicidal action. Therefore, my request to you is to create a contact information on an index card and share this card with people who care about you. Store an extra card in a place where one can easily have access to it, such as; the kitchen cabinets, at the very front of your phonebook, drawers or on your refrigerator. On the card, ensure that you clearly and correctly record the numbers of your healthcare providers, local emergency room as well as the admission personnel in the hospital who can get you quick help.

At all times, when it comes to minimizing risks, it is important to always include a suicide prevention plan together with your treatment contract. In this case, it is advisable that you work with your doctor and support team to integrate important planning component in the contract. The main reason for this is so that each person involved is aware of the warning signs that they are supposed to watch out for as well as the actions to take if they feel that you are slipping into suicidal thoughts.

Additionally, it is important for you as a bipolar disorder patient, together with your family, to be aware of the things that you should do in case of an emergency. This includes calling your doctor or making emergency arrangements with caregivers the moment you feel suicidal. Also, you can seek help from a trusted friend or family member to guard you to safety until you can get the help that you need. You can also contact emergency services whenever you think that you cannot control the feeling of harming yourself, you are hearing voices or you feel that you really want to commit suicide.

How your family can help

Your family is your support system. They play a crucial role in helping you to cope with the bipolar disorder and its symptoms. I encourage you and your family to ensure that you read this book back to back. It is especially of great importance that you review the content presented in this chapter together with your family.

The first thing that I would like you to do is to think of your family as a critical part of your treatment team. This means that you have to make a decision with them on how they can offer you their care. Ensure that they fully understand the essence of your psychiatric care. To get the best support is through effective communication between you, your family and the support team on a whole. Every single mentor and member of your support team must be on one accord to be able to accomplish effective results. It is especially crucial that all persons involved, have the same goal, which evidently, is to get you better.

Understand that when you improve communication, you are simply ensuring that you are lowering the chances of stress at home and thus boosting your relationship with your family. A tolerant and low key surrounding at home is the recipe for minimizing depressive and manic episodes of bipolar disorder. The truth is, maintaining a low atmosphere like I previously mentioned is quite challenging. It is evident that most families find it very difficult to address emotionally charged issues. This is the main reason why so many bipolar patients complain that every strong emotion they experience is attributed to their mental illness rather than what they really feel as a person. On the other hand, family members complain that the person is over-reactive about small issues and take everything to a highly emotional level. It is also a frustrating situation when most members of the support team try to evade every topic that is brought forth for discussion because they have the mindset that this is too intense for you.

A very useful and practical technique that you can employ in this case is the whisper rule. This is one of the techniques that requires the use of a simple agreement where, whenever one feels that the topic of discussion is getting supercharged, it is recommended and allowed for them to request for the discussion to be held in a whisper. However, in case this whisper rule is violated, the discussion is put out for a given period of time like 2-3 hours. In most cases, you will realize that patients who employ the use of this method in their support team often instruct their families to abide by the whisper rule to indicate that the state of their mood is normal. Additionally, the times when they fail to adhere to the whisper rule is an indication of illness.

Communication Skills

Have you ever heard of a gardener's tip? Well, when you are having a discussion with your treatment team, it pays to employ the use of this tip. The tip states that "It pays to water the flowers, not the weeds". This gardener's tip emphasizes the importance of focusing attention on what is working in the relationship and not the things that are going wrong. This means that if you want your relationship with the family and the treatment team to yield fruit, you have to ensure that the entire team is aware that you want them to do things that make you happy. Some of these things include ensuring that they remain considerate to your illness and they help at home among others. In most cases, it is quite sad that many people only pay attention to the things that are negative. They will complain about the things that are not working. It is this negative attention in most cases increase bad feelings and thus impairing with the effort to address an existing problem.

Another significant thing is that paying attention to addressing the problem is of uttermost importance when it comes to bipolar disorder patients. Problems have to be addressed once and for all. The people with bipolar disorder often do not appreciate negative feedback, as this only worsen their moods rather than help with the issues at hand. This means that effective modes of communication have to be employed.

When it comes to offering approvals to other people, family members are often inclined to giving approval to others. It is important that you use this power here! It is very critical to ensure that you appreciate the bipolar patient for the effort towards recovery by letting them know that they are on track. This is simply by giving verbal feedback, positive intonation, pleasant and appreciative eye contact, a hug, kiss, and touch among others. These are the most important strategies that you can employ to ensure that you communicate effectively and support the patient through their illness, this will be of great significance to the reduction of negative emotions.

Effective listening skills

All too often, arguments and bad attitudes arise in the family. This is frequently because of misunderstandings that revolve around what was said. The main reason for this is because each party in the conversation fails to pay attention to what the other person is saying and thus jumps into conclusions. This is what causes an emotional escalation, feelings of anger, hopelessness, and frustrations. In order to ensure that you prevent this from taking place, it is significant that each party involved in the conversation communicate with a high degree of clarity. This means that you have to get feedback to the previous message before you can communicate the second message.

Effective listening is a skill which requires that you pay attention to what is being said so that you get the accurate information from the other party. When you do this, you will simply communicate accurately to the speaker indicating in your response that you heard them loud and clear. This is what effective listening and communication skill requires. To be able to achieve this, it is important that you keep your skills and counter arguments in check long enough to ensure that you are devoted to getting the message accurately. Your role is not to give a quick response to everything that is being said. Instead, it is your responsibility to demonstrate to the person that is speaking that you heard and comprehend what they said. Once you have received the message clearly, only then can you consider giving a feedback to the message.

Some of the steps that will help you to ensure that you are effectively listening to the message that the person is trying to put across to you include the following; Giving the speaker a clear signal that you are attentive to what they are saying. The best way you can do this is simply maintaining close eye contact and nodding at every point they make. Secondly, you can ask questions in the middle of communication. This is to make the points that are being communicated clear to you.

The main goal is not to debate what is being said. Rather, it is to understand where the speaker is coming from with their argument. Thirdly, you can repeat what the speaker said back to him or her so that you can verify if what was said, was indeed what you interpreted. If the speaker is not in agreement with that, it is not important to debate what they said. The most important thing, in this case, is to have them make clarification concerning what they meant. Once both you and the speaker are in agreement with the message, then it is your turn to give a response.

Chapter 14: Management And Prognosis

Once someone has been diagnosed with borderline personality disorder, it is time to learn how to manage the disorder. It is not going to go away just because it has been diagnosed and it can take years and years of proper therapy and treatment to get the condition under control and help the person suffering from the disease learn how to live a normal life. This chapter is going to take a bit of time to look at the different types of treatments that are available to choose from and how high the success rate is for the treatments.

Management

The main treatment that people with this disorder are going to receive is psychotherapy. Usually this will either be done on its own or with one of the other methods, but there are very few times when borderline personality disorder is treated without the use of psychotherapy. The treatment that is chosen though should be completely based on the individual needs of the person at hand rather than worrying about the traditional route that might have been taken by others. Sometimes medication will be the best option, for example, because it can help to treat some of the diseases that are going to come along with this disorder.

This section will look at some of the different types of treatments that are available for this kind of disorder, how each one of them is going to work, and when each of them is going to work for your situation.

Psychotherapy

The treatment that is used the most often with borderline personality disorder is psychotherapy. This is usually going to be done for long term. There are six different types of treatments that are currently recognized for this kind of therapy for the individual. They include schema-focused therapy, general psychiatric management, dialectical behavior therapy, or DBT, transference focused psychotherapy, metallization based treatment or MBT, and dynamic deconstructive psychotherapy or DDP.

The first type of therapy we will look at is the schema focused therapy. This is the type of therapy that is used the most often for this disorder, although the others can be used just as effectively. This is an approach that is going to add some of the best things about all of the other ones and tries to combine them. The schemas in this kind of therapy are going to be the themes or patterns of thinking, behaving, and feeling that the person has been using for a long time. These will be discovered in this kind of therapy and then the clinician will be able to work with the person to get them to change the way that they look at the world. These schemas will be formed from childhood and so they are deeply rooted and will take the person a lot of time to get them to change.

This kind of therapy is going to come in three stages. The first one is considered the assessment phase where the schemas are going to be identified over the first few sessions. These will often be determined through questions to the person to get a good picture of the patterns that are involved in their thoughts. Next the doctor is going to work with the patient to bring them to the emotional awareness that they need to understand and get in touch with the schemas and then they will learn the best way to spot them in their day to day life. Finally, the stage for behavioral changes will come about and the client is going to learn how to replace the negative thoughts of the past with ones that are new and healthy.

The next type of therapy is general psychiatric management. This is the kind of therapy that you could use on almost any kind of personality disorder that there is and it is going to work to help determine what kind of disorder is present and what the person is able to do to take care of the issue. It is a long process and it is not one that is specifically made for those who have borderline personality disorder, but it can do the trick and many times it is the only option for those who do not have access to a professional on their case.

Next therapy that is often used is dialectical behavior therapy. This is quickly becoming the most popular kind of therapy that is available because it is backed by a lot of research into borderline personality disorder and is going to help the client out the most. This is often considered the most effective treatment, but it is going to take a specialist who has been trained in using it and the client must be willing to stick with it for the long term. Often this is used in a kind of group therapy to make it more effective for those who need it.

The approach that is used with this is to change the behaviors and thoughts that have been around for many years with the patient. It is also a good one to use if the client is refusing to work with the therapist for the long term because it is able to put them at ease and make them feel less like they are under attack from the therapist. This kind of therapy will be given in two components, namely individual and group therapy. In the group part, the client is going to learn the skills that they need to make their life better. During the individual sessions, the therapist is going to work with them to identify and discuss any issues that the client might have dealt with in the past week. The therapist will record these and the help to devise a plan based on how the patient is concerned about it. The therapist will also spend some time talking about life skills and issues in these sessions. This along with some training to regulate emotions is used to put the client at ease and helps them to see that there are other alternatives to dealing with their problems.

Transference focused psychotherapy is sometimes used as well. This is kind of a general term for therapy, but it is basically when the client is going to talk out their issues, problems, and feeling with their therapist. During this kind of therapy, the client is going to learn about the condition that they are in as well as their behaviors, thoughts, feelings and moods. This kind of therapy is going to help them to learn the best ways to take control in life and teach them how to respond to any situations that are challenging with the right kind of coping skills rather than letting things get out of hand.

There are a variety of different types of this therapy and all of them are going to work in different ways. Some examples of this kind of therapy will include therapy, psychosocial therapy, counseling, and talk therapy. They are meant to get the client to talk out the issues that are surrounding them to make things easier to understand and change without the confrontations that can happen with other methods.

Next is the metallization based treatment. This therapy is a kind that is used to help the client separate and differentiate their thoughts and the feelings they are having from others around them. The metallization part is the ability to understand your own behavior and feelings as well as how you are associating them with your mental states in yourself and in others.

In this therapy, the client is going to learn how to do this process by using supportive and safe methods so that they do not feel like they are attacked. This process can take some time because the person with the disorder is going to become confused when things are changed on them and not going the way that they are used to. This one is going to take a specialist to get done and could take many years to accomplish.

Finally, some clinicians will use dynamic deconstructive psychotherapy to help out those with this kind of disorder. This is a treatment that can be used is usually only going to take about 12 months to complete with the client coming in every week to get the help that they need. This kind of therapy is going to combine a lot of different elements including the deconstruction philosophy, object relations theory, and neuroscience research. The ideas behind this type of therapy state that those who have this disorder need to work on the neurocognitive deficit so that they can start to properly process their feelings when things becomes emotionally charged.

For this therapy, the patient is going to show up for weekly sessions that will last about 45 minutes. Between the sessions, the client is going to be asked to work on some special assignments each day that the therapist asks them to fill out. They are also going to be asked to work on some of their own personal relationships when they are out of the treatment. There are four stages and it is going to take 12 months. This does not mean that you will have a cured client in that 12 months, but it means that they are recovered enough to get out of such an intensive program and move on to more day to day living. If they are not to this point, the therapist will be able to block out more time to help them out.

No matter what kind of other treatment options that might be given to the patient, it is necessary for all patients to go through some form of therapy. Picking out the one that is right for the patient and is going to help them the most is the best option for everyone, but there should still be some kind of therapy present to get the best results. It is never recommended that the patient just be given medicine and then ignored because this is not going to give them the help that they need and they will never be cured.

Medications

In addition to working on therapy to help out with this disorder, some doctors may prescribe some medications to help out with the disorder. It is important to realize that medication on its own is not going to be able to help out the disorder and no one is going to get cured just by the medication that they have taken. Rather, the medication is usually used to help out with some of the underlying causes and issues that might be present so that it is easier to take care of the disorder and get the person back on the track that they belong.

There was a study done in 2010 that found that as of now there are no medications that are available for treating the core symptoms of borderline personality disorder. Even though this was found, the authors did find that some forms of medication are effective at helping the impact of some isolated symptoms or symptoms of the conditions that might be going along with the borderline personality disorder. What this means is that you are not going to be able to take a magic pill and get the results that you would like and be cured overnight, but some of the symptoms that you are feeling can be helped with medication which can make your treatment so much better in the long run.

There are some medications that you will be able to take to help with some of your symptoms. For example, haloperidol has been shown to reduce some of the anger that these clients may have and flupenthixol can reduce some of the likelihood that the client is going to have suicidal behavior. Aripiprazole can sometimes help out with the condition because it helps with anxiety, depression, paranoid symptoms, anger, impulsivity, and interpersonal problems. These are just some of the issues that medication can help with.

One of the things that medication is given out the most for when it comes to this personality disorder is the mood stabilizers. These can help out with anger, issues with relationships, anxiety, depression, and so much more. Often these are going to make it really difficult to take care of the person with the disorder and it becomes almost impossible to help them without the mood stabilizers.

Of course, the evidence that some of these medications have for helping out is a bit limited which is why some people who will not recommend these because they are worried about the safety of them. There are some guidelines in place in some countries concerning the management and treatment of this disorder. Basically, those who have the rules will say that the medications cannot be used as the sole treatment for someone who has this disorder and can only be used as part of the treatment to help along the more prominent option of therapy.

Medications are the best option if you need to deal with some of the underlying issues that are hindering the treatment of the disorder. They can take care of the other issues so that you are able to concentrate more on the treatment for your personality disorder. It is important that the medications are never taken on their own though and it is best to have them just as the supplement to the therapy to get the best treatment for all around. This will ensure that the patient is getting the best care, being monitored when needed, and that they can get off the medication as soon as it is no longer providing them with the benefits and care that it was meant for.

Services

While anyone who has this disorder is going to be able to benefit from treatment and getting the help that is available from a therapist or other doctor, most of those with this disorder are never going to get the help that they need. This is because most of them will not realize that they have an issue and the rest will not admit that they have an issue and will never seek the treatment that they need. Even for those who go and get the treatment that they need, it is hard to find a doctor who is going to be able to help them out the right way and they are not going to be able to get the good treatments that are available to some.

It is difficult for those who need to get the treatment to find the treatment options that they need. This is because of their location, the fact that they will need to be able to find the money to do treatments that they need and so they will take lower programs that will cost them less, and the fact that the services that they are going to receive will vary between the places that they get.

Managing the treatment of this disorder is going to be really tough. It is not something that can be done in just a short period of time and often it can take many years and a combination of different therapies and drugs to get it figured out. The client also needs to be willing to trust the clinician and stick with the treatment for a number of years, something that is difficult for someone with borderline personality disorder to properly do.

Prognosis

Out of those who get the treatment that they are needing when suffering from this disorder, the majority are going to do well and can get some relief from their symptoms and they will go into remission for at least two years if not longer. This is for those who went through the proper treatments and who stuck with it for the length of time that was required, something that is hard to get done for a person with borderline personality disorder.

According to a study that was done to track the symptoms of those who had this disorder and got the proper treatment, about 34 percent were in remission within two years of starting their treatment. After four years, this number went up to almost 50 percent and then within six years it was almost to 60 percent. By the end of this study, almost 74 percent of the participants were in remission. Out of those who had gotten to the recovery phase, less than 6 percent had gone backwards and began to see the same issues as they had before when they had the disorder. Another study that was done later found that after ten years of therapy and a change in lifestyle, a good 86 percent of the patients had gotten to a stable recovery from their symptoms.

What this shows you is that the majority of those who have undergone treatment are going to be able to see the results that they want as long as they are able to stick with the program and the amount of time that they have to spend in the program is going to vary depending on a variety of factors. Of course, there are some people who are not able to succeed in their goals and they are not going to be able to get through the therapy. Many times these people may not trust their therapist, may not see that there is a problem, or they were not able to stay for the length of the program to see the results of the participation.

These findings are contrary to what a lot of people have believed for many years. For a long time, people thought that it was impossible to get over borderline personality disorder, but with the right amount of treatment and time, it is possible to help reverse how these clients act in their world, even when they have some of the worst symptoms. These kinds of relief form the symptoms are only going to be possible for those who get treatment, regardless of the type and those who never receive treatment are not going to see the results that they would like.

Conclusion

Thanks again for downloading this book!

Psychiatric disorders like bipolar disorder can become very crippling especially if patients don't get the support they need from friends and family. Misunderstanding their condition can further isolate them and worsen their episodes of mania and depression.

Bipolar disorder is not an abnormality. It is a psychological condition often caused by various factors. While it is often a long-term struggle, bipolar patients can be cured through the help of psychotherapy and psychiatric medication, especially if done as often as possible.

If you or someone you love suffers from manic depression, I hope this book was able to help you understand this medical ailment better. Remember that there is always hope for full recovery and treatment or at the very least to make the episodes less frequent and more manageable for patients.

However, whether it's just a mild case of bipolar disorder or an extreme one, it's always recommended that you consult with a medical professional who specializes in psychiatric cases. Do no leave anything to chance; you might do more harm than good when you attempt to self-medicate to treat a serious psychiatric disorder such as manic depression.

Even if you've finished reading this book, please make sure you take the necessary steps toward ensuring that bipolar patients get the right kind of medical attention as well as the full love and support of the people around them. Also, do not wait for the condition to reach a more serious stage before you take action. By the time you deem the condition is serious enough to be treated, it may already be too late for you or your loved one.

Thank you and good luck!